ABC-123 PICTURE BOOK

By Thomas Bangert
Illustrated by Teagan White

OneBillionSEEDS
SANTA MONICA, CALIFORNIA

"I have great faith in a seed."
–Henry David Thoreau

To my grandmother, Margaret Rose, for growing my imagination.

Copyright © 2016 by Thomas Bangert

All rights reserved. No part of this publication may be reproduced or transmitted in any form or by any means, electronic or mechanical, including photocopy, recording, or any information storage and retrieval system, without permission in writing from the publisher.

Requests for permission to make copies of any part of the work should be submitted online at www.OneBillionSEEDS.com/contact or mailed to the following address: Permissions Department, OneBillionSEEDS LLC, 171 Pier Avenue NO. 415, Santa Monica, CA 90405.

www.OneBillionSEEDS.com   www.GrowPrepareShare.com   www.FarmFoodFRIENDS.com

Special thanks to Eze Blaine, Design/Brand Consultant

One Billion Seeds, Grow Prepare Share, and Farm Food Friends are registered trademarks of OneBillionSEEDS LLC.

ISBN 978-0-692-26586-4

Designed in California, USA

How to Use This Book

Recognizing letters and numbers is the most important pre-school skill parents and families can help children learn. FarmFoodFRIENDS ABC-123 Picture Book features 26 beautifully illustrated watercolor farm scenes that help children learn the alphabet, numbers, vocabulary, writing, and where food comes from on a farm.

Parents and teachers may use this book to introduce children and English learners to the letters Aa-Zz, the counting numbers 1-26, primary writing sentences, positive personality traits, and smiling farm food characters for imagination and story telling. There is also a Glossary of the 26 fruits and vegetables, along with each character's positive personality trait, to get the conversations started! Please visit our website:

www.FarmFoodFRIENDS.com

About OneBillionSEEDS

OneBillionSEEDS is an education company with a global vision of teaching and facilitating language development through food. We have created a platform for parents and teachers to help their children learn fundamental language that promotes literacy and imagination through food, and the understanding of where food comes from on a farm. Our group of original characters is called the Farm Food Friends, consisting of an equal amount of boy and girl farm food characters. The characters live on a farm that is designed with a polyculture and permaculture system...they benefit each other, and have a positive personality trait that can be reflected upon and talked about for years to come. OneBillionSEEDS promotes a simple paradigm called GPS... GROW PREPARE SHARE. We want children to learn to GROW their own food, PREPARE their own meals, and SHARE what they create!

One Billion Seeds, Grow Prepare Share, and Farm Food Friends are registered trademarks of OneBillionSEEDS LLC.

I is adventurous.

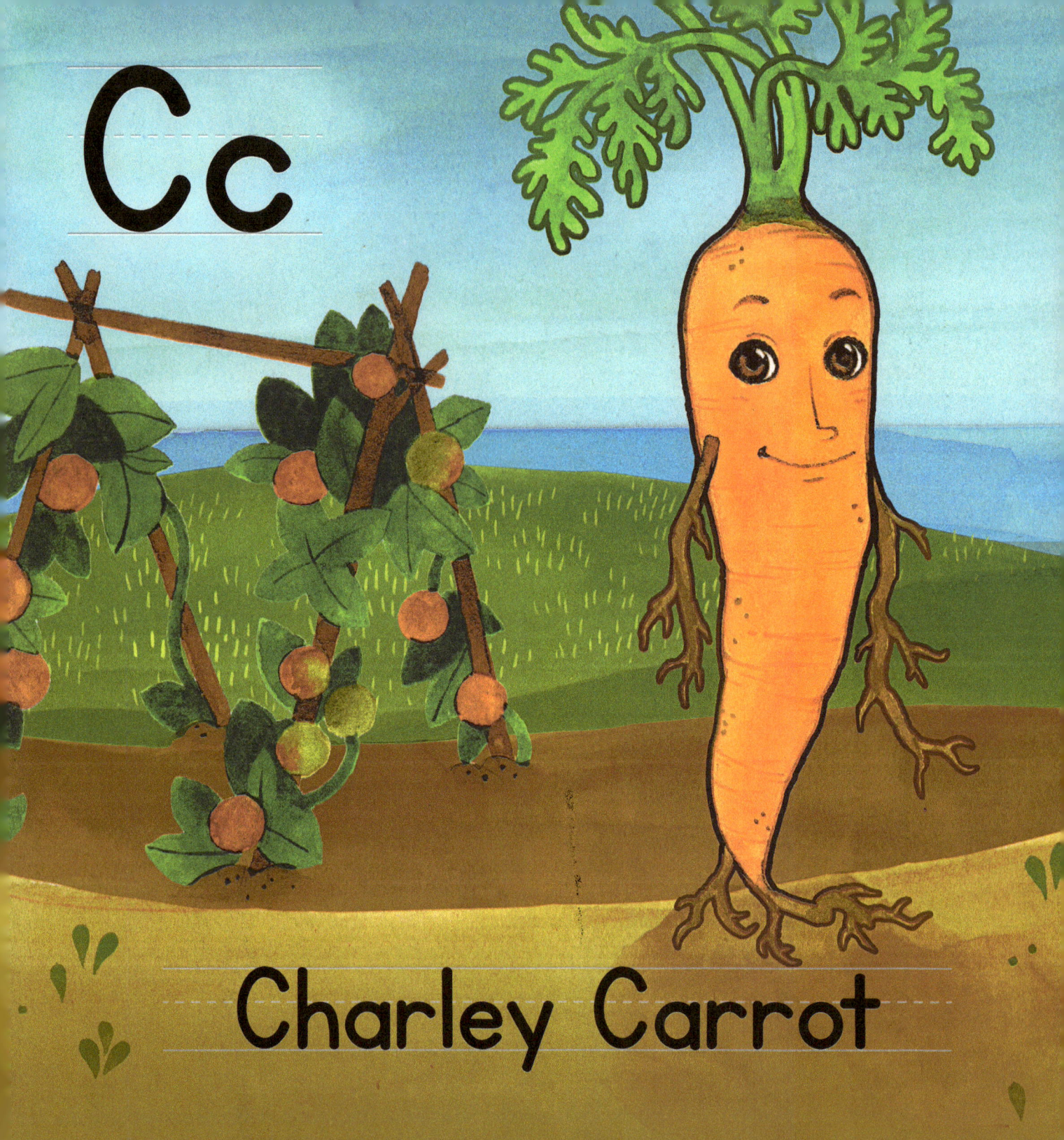

3

is caring.

4

_____ is dynamic.

5

_____ is energetic.

7

is generous.

is happy.

q is imaginative.

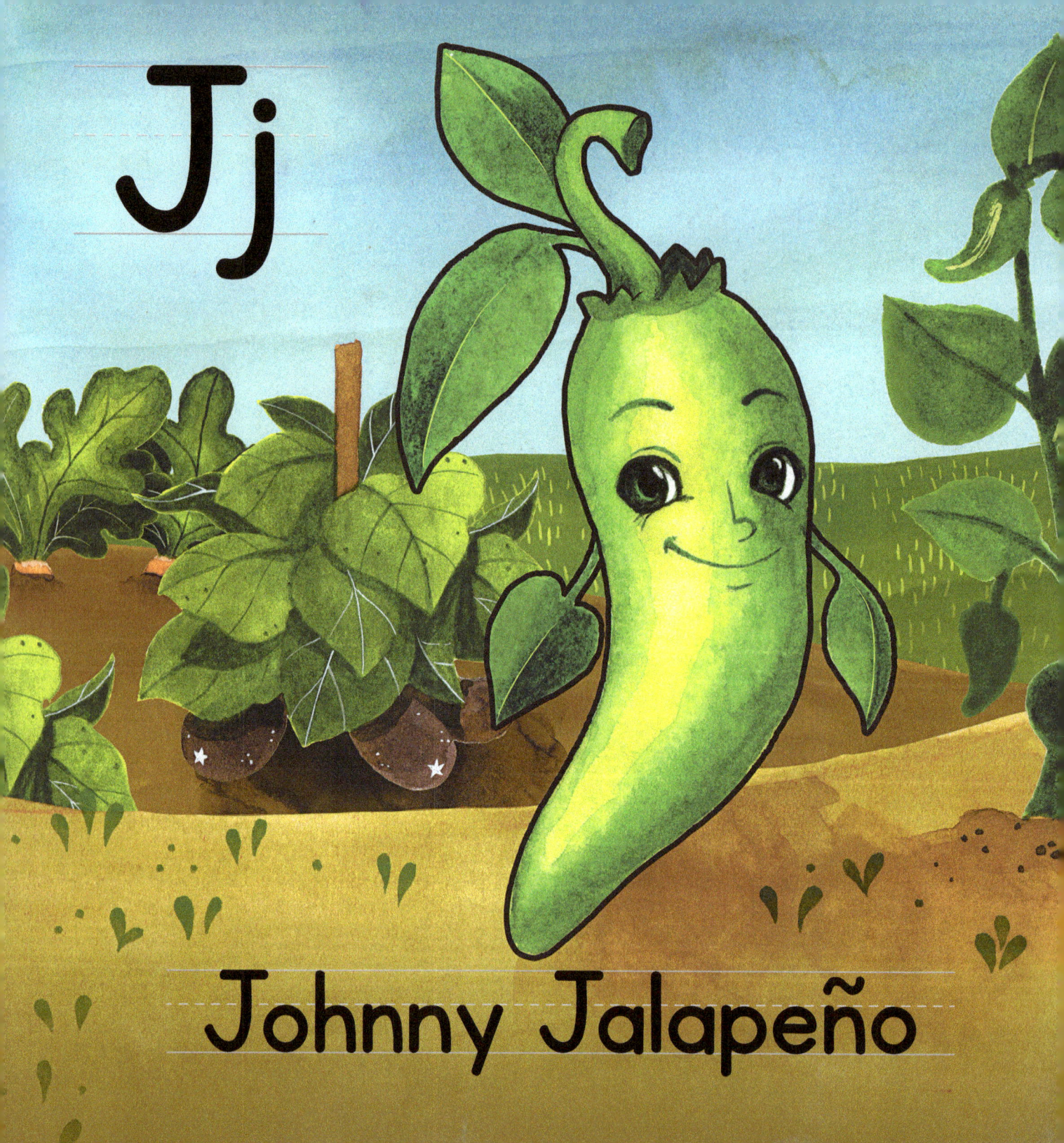

10

is jolly.

12

_____ is loyal.

14
_____ is nurturing.

15

_____ is optimistic.

16

___ is passionate.

18

_____ is responsible.

19

is spiritual.

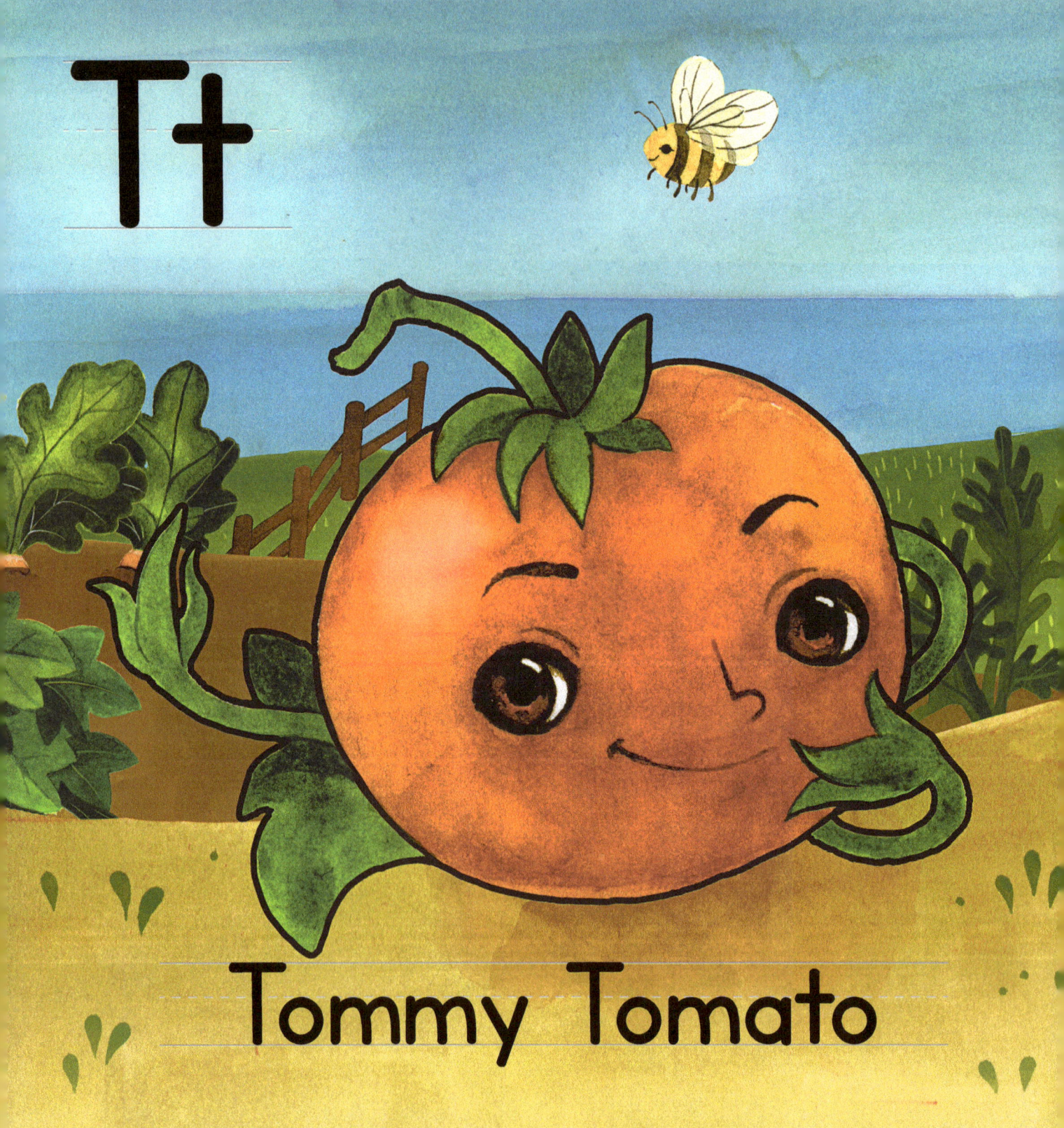

20

____ is thoughtful.

Uu

Una Ugli

21

_____ is unique.

24

is xenophilic.

25

is yielding.

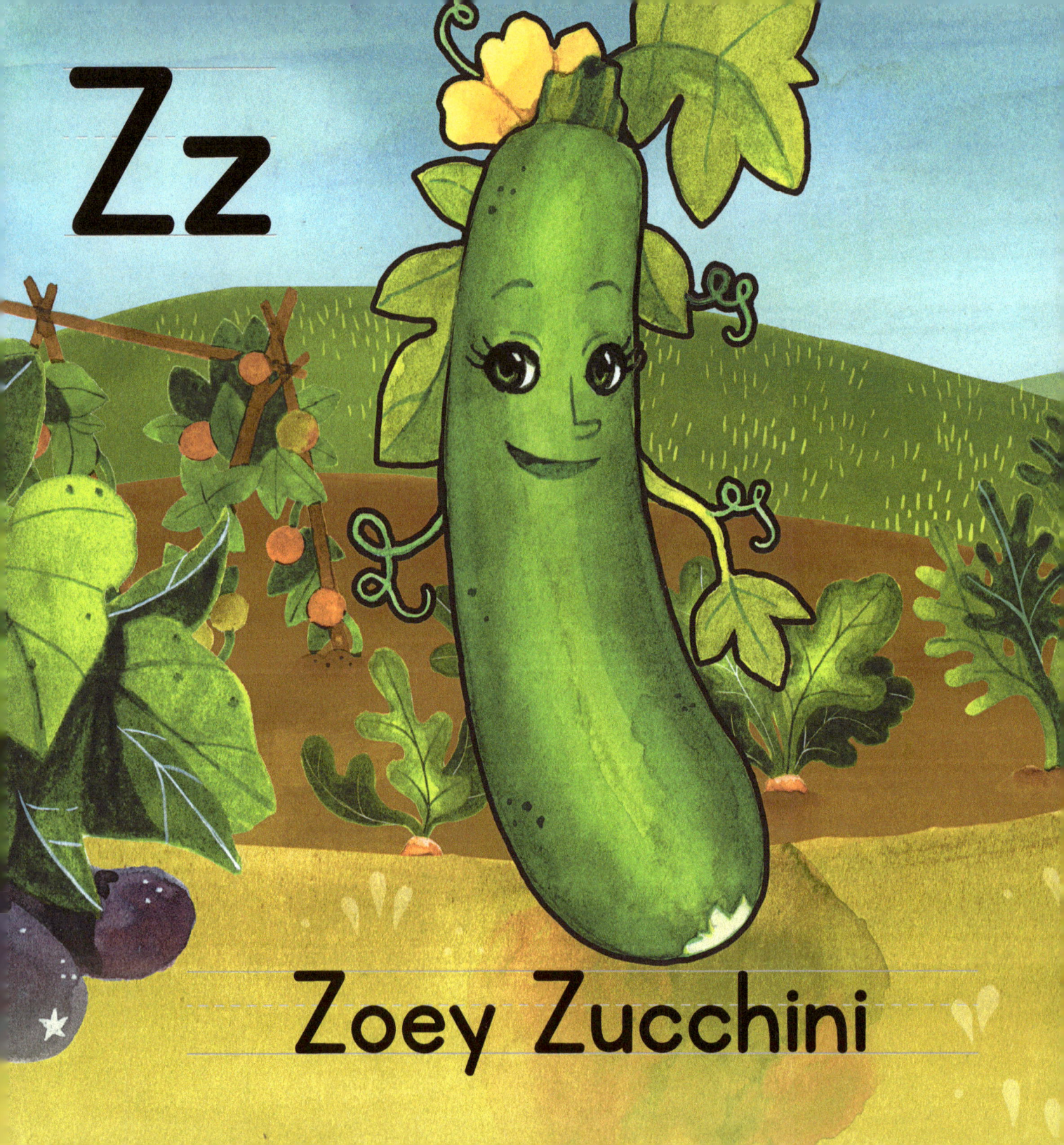

is zingy.

Glossary

26 Fruits & Vegetables + Positive Personality Traits to Talk About...

Ava Apple (ap·ple):
a rounded tree fruit with a red, yollow, or green skin, firm white flesh and a seedy core
Adventurous (ad·ven·tur·ous):
ready to take risks or to deal with the new and unknown, a willingness to accept risks but does not rule out showing good sense

Benny Banana (ba·nana):
a treelike tropical plant with larger leaves and flower clusters that develop into a bunch of finger-shaped fruit which are usually yellow when ripe
Brave (brave):
feeling or displaying no fear, ready to face or bear with, and show courage

Charley Carrot (car·rot):
the long orange edible root of a common garden plant that is eaten as a vegetable
Caring (car·ing):
to feel interest or concern for others, displaying kindness

Desi Date (date):
the oblong edible tree fruit of a tall Old World palm
Dynamic (dy·nam·ic):
marked by continuous progress, activity, or change,
positive in attitude and full of energy and new ideas

Emma Eggplant (egg·plant):
a widely cultivated herb that is related to the potato and
yields edible fruit
Energetic (en·er·get·ic):
having or showing energy, great activity, or vitality

Fernie Fig (fig):
an edible tree fruit that is oblong or shaped like a pear and grows
on a tree related to the mulberries
Friendly (friend·ly):
showing kindly interest and goodwill, bringing comfort or
cheer on good or affectionate terms

Gino Garlic (gar·lic):
a European herb related to onion and grown for its bulbs that have
a strong smell and taste and are used to flavor foods
Generous (gen·er·ous):
free in giving or sharing, showing kindness toward others

Hanna Honeydew (honey·dew):
vines of pale smooth-skinned muskmelon with greenish sweet flesh
Happy (hap·py):
enjoying well-being and contentment, being pleased or glad, having a sense of confidence or satisfaction

Isabella Iceberg (ice·berg):
a lettuce with a tight round head of light green crisp leaves
Imaginative (imag·i·na·tive):
the act, process, or power of forming a mental picture of something not present and especially of something one has not known or experienced, a creation of the mind, having or showing creativity or inventiveness

Johnny Jalapeño (jala·peño):
a medium-sized chili pepper
Jolly (jol·ly):
merry, cheerful, happy, very pleasant or agreeable

Kelly Kiwi (ki·wi):
the edible fruit of a Chinese vine having a fuzzy brown skin and sligthly tart green flesh
Kind (kind):
wanting and liking to do good and to bring happiness to others, showing or growing out of gentleness or goodness of heart, having or showing a friendly, generous, and considerate nature

Lucy Lemon (lem·on):
a yellow oblong fruit with sour juice and a thick rind from which a fragrant oil is obtained
Loyal (loy·al):
giving or showing firm and constant support or allegiance to a person or institution, faithful to one's lawful government, faithful to a person to whom allegiance or affection is due, faithful to a cause or ideal

Manny Mango (man·go):
a yellowish red tropical fruit with a firm skin, hard central stony seed, and juicy mildly tart pulp
Motivating (mo·ti·vat·ing):
to provide with a reason for doing something, stimulate (someone's) interest in our enthusiasm for doing something

Natalie Nectarine (nec·tar·ine):
a smooth-skinned peach
Nurturing (nur·tur·ing):
educate, to further the development of, care for and encourage the growth of

Olivia Olive (ol·ive):
a Mediterranean evergreen tree grown for its fruit and oil
Optimistic (op·ti·mis·tic):
expecting everything to come out all right, hopeful and confident about the future

Priscilla Pumpkin (pump·kin):
the usually round orange fruit of a vine of the gourd family widely used as food
Passionate (pas·sion·ate):
excited or easily excited to strong feeling, showing or expressing strong feelings or a strong belief

Quincy Quince (quince):
the fruit of an Asian tree that resembles a yellow apple with hard flesh and is used especially for marmalade, jelly, and preserves
Quick (quick):
fast in understanding, thinking, or learning, mentally keen, reacting with speed and alertness, prompt to understand, think, or learn; intelligent

Raoul Radish (rad·ish):
the crisp edible root of a plant related to the mustards that is usually eaten raw as a vegetable
Responsible (re·spon·si·ble):
being the one who must answer or account for something, being the cause or explanation, able to choose for oneself between right and wrong, to take charge of or be trusted with important matters, having an obligation to do something, or having control over or care for
someone, as part of one's job or role

Sunshine Sunflower (sun·flow·er):
any of a genus of tall herbs that are often grown for their large showy flower heads with yellow ray flowers and for their oil-rich seeds
Spiritual (spir·i·tu·al):
of, relating to, or consisting of spirit : not bodily or material, not concerned with material values or pursuits

Tommy Tomato (to·ma·to):
a usually large rounded red or sometimes yellow pulpy berry that is eaten as a vegetable
Thoughtful (thought·ful):
marked by careful thinking, considerate of the needs of others

Una Ugli (ugli):
a Jamaican mottled green and yellow citrus fruit that is a hybrid of grapefruit and tangerine
Unique (unique):
being the only one of its kind, unlike anything else, particularly remarkable, special

Veronica Voavanga (vo·a·van·ga):
the Spanish tamarind is a round fruit, that is green with white dots, and that turns brown when fully ripe
Virtuous (vir·tu·ous):
having or showing high moral standards, conduct that agrees with what is morally right

Willy Watermelon (wa·ter·mel·on):
the large fruit of a plant of the gourd family, with smooth green skin, red pulp, and sweet watery juice
Wise (wise):
having or showing experience, wisdom, good sense, or good judgment

Xavier Xigua (she·gwah):
the Mandarin Chinese word for watermelon
Xenophilic (xen·o·phil·ic):
an attraction to foreign peoples, cultures, customs or manners

Youmee Yam (yam):
the edible starchy tuber of a climbing plant, widely distributed in tropical and subtropical countries
Yielding (yield·ing):
not rigid or stiff, tending to give in to the wishes of another

Zoey Zucchini (zuc·chi·ni):
a green variety of smooth-skinned summer squash
Zingy (zing·y):
energy, enthusiasm, or liveliness, enjoyably exciting, strikingly attractive or appealing

Glossary
Creatures on the Farm

 Eimear the European Honey Bee

 Goldie the Goldfinch Bird

 Martha the Mexican Monarch Butterfly

 Chow (Summer) & Chyou (Autumn) the Chinese Silkie Chickens

 Sandy the Scottish Highland Cow

 Catalina & Cruz the Spanish Goats

 Brendan the Irish Bog Pony

www.ingramcontent.com/pod-product-compliance
Lightning Source LLC
Chambersburg PA
CBHW061814290426
44110CB00026B/2874